For Nancy, Yudai, Ayako, and the whole McClendon Clan

Zyaoi Media Books

Nana the Happy Face Spider's
Happy, Sad, Happy Day!
Illustrated By Eunice Kim & Allen Liu
Written By David A. Oglesby

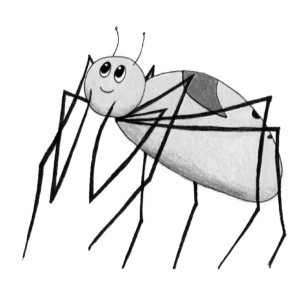

Zyaoi Media Books

One fine Hawaiian morning, high on a mountain range, on the island of Oahu, a young Happy Face Spider named Nana woke up very, _VERY_ HAPPY!

She was happy because it was her birthday! "What's going to happen?" she wondered.

"Where is everyone?" she thought. As she looked around her web, leaf, and tree there was no one to be found.

"Hello?" she called out. There was no answer.
"Maybe they went to get some yummy food."

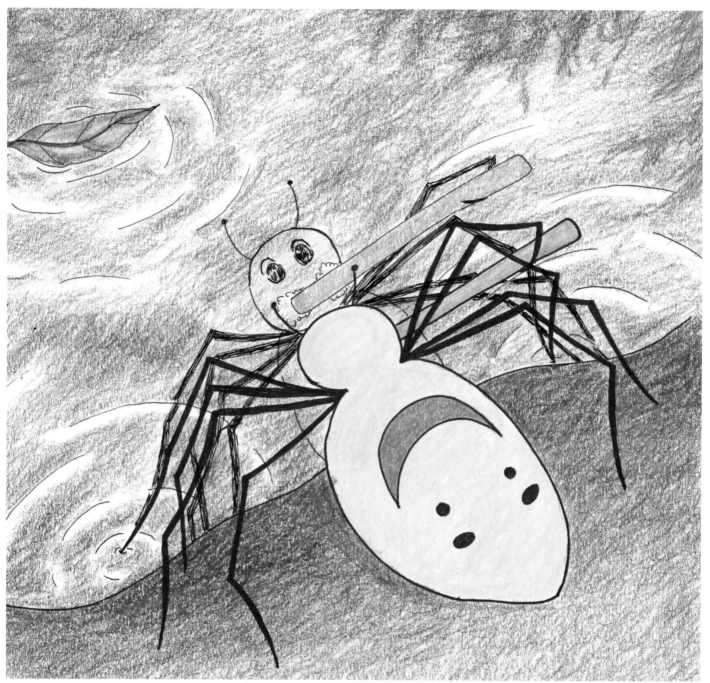

Excited, she quickly washed her face and brushed her teeth.
Then she left her tree, looking for her family and friends.

In the grass next to her home lived Pueo, her friend, the Hawaiian Owl. "Pueo" she called; "Are you there?"

No one answered. "Interesting," she thought, "Pueo is usually resting at this hour. She is a night owl. Where could she be?"

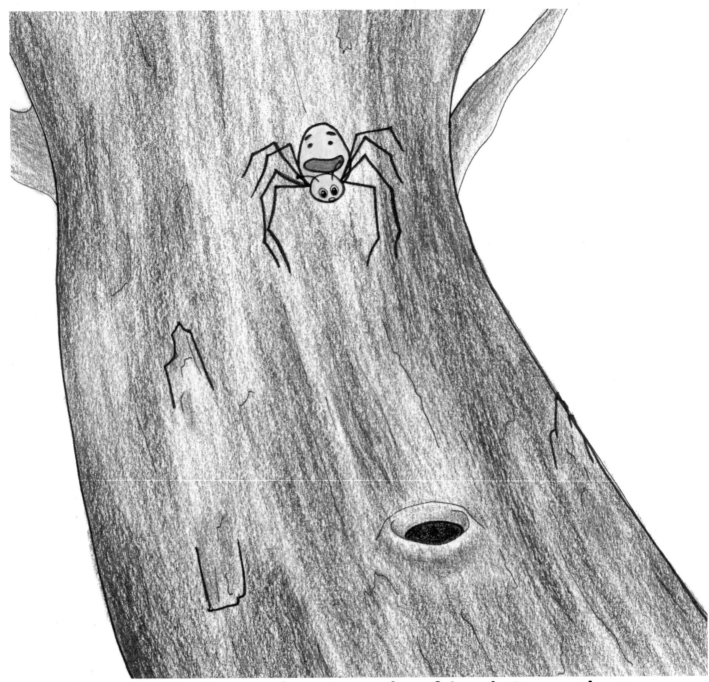

Nana decided to seek out another friend, Pupu, the tree snail. She scurried up Pupu's tree to look into his home. "Pupu? Pupu?"

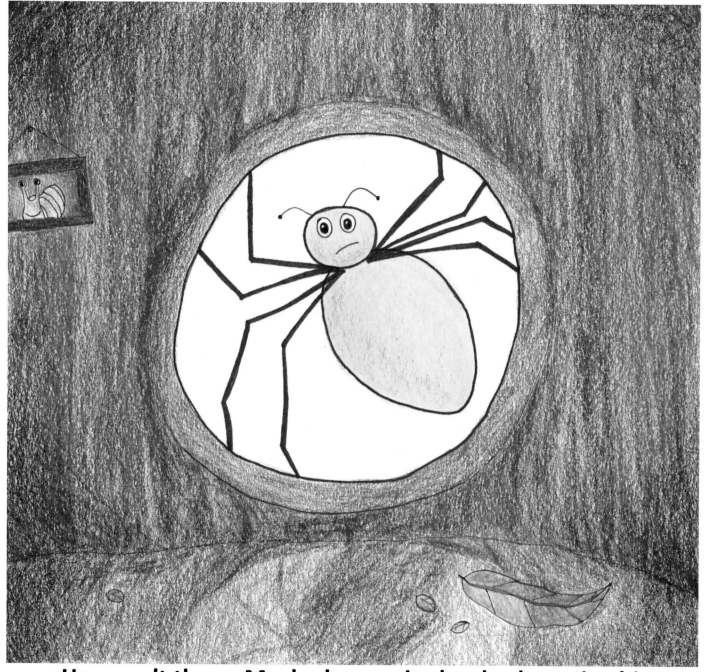

He wasn't there. Maybe he was in the shrubs eating his
favorite fungus. Pupu knew today was her birthday;
so where could he be?

Then she thought, "Maybe Pueo and Pupu are with our *other* friend, Kane, the Kamehameha butterfly." Nana went to Kane's nettle patch hoping to find everyone.

Unfortunately, no one was around...

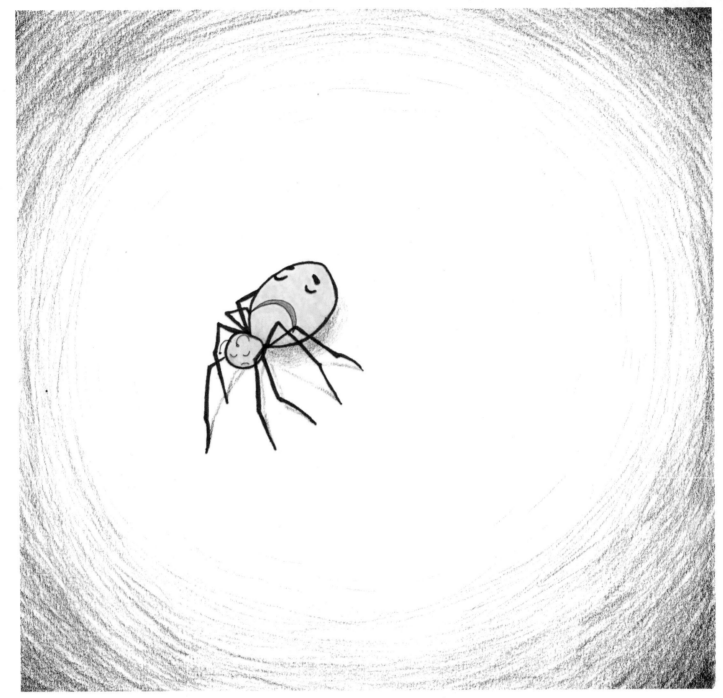

Now, Nana was sad. She was very, *VERY* sad!

When she arrived at her tree, she saw the wise old crow,
'Alalā. 'Alalā could tell that Nana was *NOT* happy and asked,
"Nana, what's wrong?"

Nana replied; "I'm very, *VERY* sad." "It's my birthday and no one is here to celebrate with me."

Nana said, "I've never flown before. Is it safe?"
'Alalā replied; "Is it *safe*?", laughing a little, "Of course,
I do it every day." Nana answered; "Well… OK."

"Are you ready?"

"YES!"

"Here we GOOOOO!"
    The air goes *Swoosh!* as they fly above the trees.

"Wow, it's so beautiful. What's that over there?"

"That's Diamond Head and the Pacific Ocean."

"How about over there?"

"That's Aloha Tower and the pier."

"This is amazing! I *love* flying!" Nana exclaimed.

After a few twists and turns, ʻAlalā swung back
towards a patch of trees.

'Alalā shouted, "Oh, look. Who's that over there?"

Nana looked and saw her family and friends.

When ʻAlalā landed, everyone cheered and shouted:
"HAPPY BIRTHDAY!"

Nana greeted everyone and she was no longer very, very sad...

...but very, *VERY* HAPPY!

Made in the USA
San Bernardino, CA
07 August 2020

76338107R00018